Responsible

Building Trust and Mitigating Risks

Taylor Royce

DEDICATION

The innovators, philosophers, and leaders who work to turn artificial intelligence into a positive force are honored in this book. To individuals who are dedicated to making sure AI is created, used, and regulated in a way that respects human dignity, privacy, and equity.

I hope this work encourages everyone influencing technology to do so with the discernment, moral character, and vision required to create a future in which artificial intelligence works best for humanity. To the ethical, open, and responsible AI of the future.

DISCLAIMER

This book's content is intended solely for general informative purposes. Although every attempt has been taken to guarantee the content's accuracy and dependability, the author and publisher make no explicit or implicit guarantees or warranties about the content's completeness, accuracy, or dependability.

Readers should seek the assistance of qualified specialists for advice particular to their requirements or circumstances, as the information is not meant to be used as legal, financial, or professional advice. The publisher and author disclaim all responsibility for any harm or loss resulting from the use of the data in this book.

The thoughts and viewpoints presented in this book are those of the author and may not represent those of any institutions, organizations, or other entities that the author may be connected to. Although the case studies and examples in this book are meant to offer background and understanding, they should not be interpreted as recommendations or assurances of success in comparable circumstances.

You understand and accept these terms by reading this book.

CONTENTS

ACKNOWLEDGMENTS..1

CHAPTER 1...1

Comprehending Platforms for AI Governance..........................1

   1.1 The AI Governance Concept..1

   1.2 Structures for AI Accountability and Trust.......................3

   1.3 Essential Elements of Platforms for AI Governance........4

CHAPTER 2...8

The Ethical and Legal Aspects of AI Governance.....................8

   2.1 Adherence to Regulations...8

   2.2 Deploying AI Ethically...10

   2.3 Mechanisms for Accountability......................................12

CHAPTER 3...15

Establishing Transparency to Foster Trust.............................15

   3.1 AI Systems Explainability...15

   3.2 Open Communication and Reporting..............................17

   3.3 Establishing Trust with Stakeholders.............................19

CHAPTER 4...23

AI Systems Risk Management...23

   4.1 Recognizing AI Dangers...23

   4.2 Operational Risk Mitigation...26

   4.3 Handling Risks to Reputation...29

CHAPTER 5...33

Putting AI Governance Policies into Practice..........................33

5.1 Creating Successful Policies..33

5.2 Putting Governance Platforms into Practice....................36

5.3 Observation and Assessment...38

CHAPTER 6..**43**

Data Privacy and AI Governance..**43**

6.1 AI and Data Protection Laws...43

6.2 Handling Private Information..46

6.3 Harmonizing Privacy and Innovation................................49

CHAPTER 7..**54**

Governance of AI through Ethical Frameworks..................**54**

7.1 Responsible AI Principles...54

7.2 Guidelines and Standards for the Industry.......................57

7.3 Encouraging Inclusion and Diversity in AI......................60

CHAPTER 8..**64**

AI Governance Platform Trends for the Future..................**64**

8.1 Advances in Technology for Governance...........................64

8.2 AI Lifecycle Management Integration................................68

8.3 Getting Ready for Changing Regulatory Environments...71

CHAPTER 9..**75**

Real-World Applications and Case Studies...........................**75**

9.1 Healthcare AI Governance..75

9.2 Governance of the Financial Sector...................................78

9.3 Applications of AI Governance in the Public Sector.......81

CHAPTER 10..**85**

AI Governance's Opportunities and Challenges...................**85**

10.1 Overcoming Obstacles in Implementation........................85

10.2 Assessing Governance Success.....................................89

10.3 Prospects for International Cooperation.........................92

ABOUT THE AUTHOR..96

ACKNOWLEDGMENTS

My sincere appreciation goes out to everyone who helped me along the way as I wrote this book. It has been a difficult but worthwhile road to write **Responsible AI: Building Trust and Mitigating Risks,** and it would not have been possible without the support, knowledge, and contributions of many amazing people.

I want to start by expressing my gratitude to my family and friends for their unwavering belief in and support of my initiative. Your tolerance, comprehension, and unwavering support have been priceless.

The foundation of this book has been shaped by the research, insights, and creative ideas of thought leaders and specialists in the fields of governance and artificial intelligence. I'm motivated by your efforts to go deeper and more clearly into the nuances of AI governance.

Additionally, I would like to thank the publishers, editors, and designers who put in many hours to make this book a reality. This book is of the greatest caliber because to your expertise and meticulous attention to detail.

Last but not least, I want to thank the innumerable people and institutions striving for the responsible advancement and application of AI technologies. Your commitment to moral innovation and constructive social effect is what keeps motivating and advancing this profession.

This book is for everyone who is dedicated to transforming AI into a positive force that works for humanity in a transparent, equitable, and responsible manner. We appreciate all of your visible and invisible contributions that helped make this a reality.

CHAPTER 1

COMPREHENDING PLATFORMS FOR AI GOVERNANCE

Platforms for AI governance are essential to guaranteeing the moral, open, and efficient application of AI systems. Building trust, reducing risks, and bringing technology developments into line with social values all depend on the ethical application of AI as it permeates industries. The fundamental components of AI governance platforms are broken down in this chapter, providing insights into their significance and functionality.

1.1 The AI Governance Concept

AI Governance: Definition and Scope

The structures, rules, and procedures intended to supervise the creation, application, and continuous administration of AI systems are collectively referred to as AI governance. It protects the public's trust while making sure that these technologies follow the law, ethical norms, and operational requirements.

1. **The following are important facets of AI governance: Ethical Oversight:** Making sure AI complies with social standards and human rights.
2. Respecting laws and regulations, such as the GDPR for data protection or industry-specific rules like those pertaining to healthcare and finance, is known as "Regulatory Compliance."
3. **Risk Mitigation:** Recognizing and resolving possible negative effects, such as prejudice, false information, and security flaws.
4. Preserving the dependability, precision, and effectiveness of AI outputs is known as "operational integrity."

Value in Overcoming Obstacles

Although they can increase societal benefits, AI systems can sometimes be dangerous. Governance offers a methodical approach to these issues:

- **Legal:** Limiting liability and making sure systems adhere to changing rules.
- **Ethical:** Preventing harm by integrating

accountability, inclusivity, and fairness into the development and application of AI.

- **Operational:** Increasing credibility with clear procedures and strong performance indicators.

1.2 Structures for AI Accountability and Trust

Overarching Guidelines for Building AI System Trust When systems are:

- **Transparent**: Users and stakeholders can comprehend the decision-making process, trust in AI is established.
- **Fair:** Discriminatory outcomes are avoided by systems.
- **Reliable:** AI constantly operates as planned in a variety of scenarios.
- **Secure:** Privacy and data integrity are safeguarded.

These ideas are put into practice by governance platforms, which offer resources for:

- Finding and reducing bias in training datasets and algorithms is known as **Bias Detection.**
- **Explainability**: Providing information about the

decision-making process of AI models.

- Regularly evaluating and verifying system outputs against benchmarks is known as performance auditing.

Consistency with Operational and Ethical Objectives

Platforms for AI governance act as a link between lofty moral ideals and realistic business objectives. For example:

Ethical Objective: Preserve user privacy.

- Protocols for encryption and data anonymization serve as the operational mechanism.

Ethical Objective: Assure equity.

- **Operational Mechanism:** Using different datasets and bias-mitigation techniques.

Successful platforms combine these objectives into a coherent framework, allowing businesses to create AI systems that are both highly effective and socially conscious.

1.3 Essential Elements of Platforms for AI Governance

Tools for Policy Creation and Management

Centralized resources for creating, executing, and revising AI policies are provided by governance platforms. With the aid of these technologies, companies can:

- Identify appropriate AI use cases.
- Provide rules for sharing, storing, and using data.
- Describe the procedures for adhering to local, national, and international laws.

A governance platform might, for instance, offer editable models for AI ethical rules or data protection policies that are suited to particular sectors, such as healthcare or finance.

Capabilities for Monitoring and Reporting

The integrity of AI systems must be continuously monitored. Among the main characteristics of monitoring and reporting tools are:

- **Real-Time Analytics:** Monitoring AI performance indicators and identifying irregularities.
- **Incident Reporting:** Recording departures from the norm, like security lapses or problems relating to bias.
- **Compliance Dashboards:** Illustrating how AI

systems conform to rules and guidelines.

By having these capabilities, businesses may minimize risks and preserve stakeholder trust by being able to react proactively to possible problems.

Accountability and Transparency Facilitators

The cornerstones of governance are accountability and transparency. Platforms improve these attributes by:

- **Model Documentation:** Documenting the AI system's design, training, and deployment procedures.
- **Decision Logging:** Keeping thorough records of AI choices to aid with user inquiries and audits.
- **Stakeholder Communication Tools:** Giving non-technical audiences concise explanations of AI procedures and outcomes.

These enablers ensure that AI systems function responsibly and successfully by promoting transparency, which in turn builds trust among users, regulators, and the general public.

This chapter provides a solid foundation for understanding

AI governance platforms and emphasizes their critical function in developing reliable, moral, and functional AI systems.

CHAPTER 2

THE ETHICAL AND LEGAL ASPECTS OF AI GOVERNANCE

Because artificial intelligence (AI) is developing so quickly, a strong framework is needed to make sure that its creation and application respect ethical standards, legal constraints, and society norms. Building trust, avoiding harm, and optimizing benefits all depend on the legal and ethical aspects of AI governance. As the cornerstones of responsible AI governance, this chapter explores accountability procedures, ethical AI deployment, and regulatory compliance.

2.1 Adherence to Regulations

Important International Laws Affecting AI Governance
National, regional, and worldwide legal frameworks must all be followed when governing AI. These rules cover a range of topics related to AI use, including algorithmic accountability and data protection.

Among the noteworthy rules are:

- **General Data Protection Regulation (GDPR):** A pillar of data privacy legislation, GDPR requires transparency in the gathering and use of data, especially for AI systems that handle personal data.

- The European Union proposed the Artificial Intelligence Act (EU AI Act), which places stringent requirements on high-risk applications such as biometric identification and classifies AI systems according to risk levels (e.g., high-risk, low-risk).

- Organizations must evaluate and reduce the risks of prejudice and discrimination in automated systems under the Algorithmic Accountability Act (USA).

- **The AI Governance Principles of China:** emphasizes encouraging innovation while maintaining safety, equity, and conformity to moral principles.

Governance Platforms' Function in Fulfilling Compliance Needs

By serving as go-betweens, governance platforms convert legislative directives into workable rules and guidelines.

They offer resources to:

- **Automate Compliance Checks:** To detect non-compliance early, regularly assess AI systems against regulatory criteria.
- **Preserve Audit Records:** To ensure traceability and preparedness for external audits, document each step of AI development and implementation.
- **Adapt to Evolving Laws:** Modify frameworks on the fly to account for modifications to rules.

A GDPR compliance module, for instance, that monitors data usage, offers data subject access reports, and guarantees lawful processing might be included in a governance platform.

2.2 Deploying AI Ethically

The difficulties in guaranteeing equity, fairness, and nondiscrimination

Despite their strength, AI systems are vulnerable to biases present in their design or training data. These biases have the potential to undermine public trust and sustain inequality if they are not addressed.

Some of the main obstacles are:

- **Training Data Bias:** Results may be skewed by historical injustices or unrepresentative datasets, which disadvantage some populations.

- **Algorithmic Transparency:** Deep learning and other complex models can act as "black boxes," hiding the reasoning behind choices.

- **Global Variability:** It is challenging to attain universal justice due to cultural and regional variations in ethical norms.

Bias Detection and Mitigation Tools

Platforms for governance include sophisticated mechanisms to handle these issues:

- **Bias Auditing:** Algorithms look for skewed representation in datasets and highlight areas that need attention.

- **Fairness Metrics:** Tools determine fairness indices, guaranteeing that all demographics are treated equally.

- **Ethical Guidelines Templates:** Organizations can create and operationalize ethical principles with the use of predefined frameworks.

- Reweighting datasets, using adversarial debiasing methods, and adding counterfactual data points are examples of mitigation techniques.

Fairness tools, for instance, can model different situations to see if an AI system consistently makes choices for a range of groups, pointing out inconsistencies for improvement.

2.3 Mechanisms for Accountability

Explainability is crucial for decision-making systems.
The ability of AI systems to communicate the logic behind their choices in a form that is understandable to humans is known as explainability. This is especially important in high-stakes fields like law enforcement, healthcare, and finance.

Advantages of Explainability:

- **Building Trust:** When stakeholders comprehend the reasoning behind AI decisions, they are more inclined to accept them.

- **Encouraging Compliance:** A number of laws, including the GDPR, mandate that people have the right to know how AI affects them.
- **Improving System Reliability:** Explainability helps find error or discrepancy in AI models.

Explainability is made possible by governance platforms in the following ways:

- **Natural Language Explanations:** Transforming algorithmic reasoning into language that is understandable by humans.
- **Visual Models:** Offering visual representations such as feature significance graphs or decision trees.
- **Interactive Dashboards:** Enable stakeholders to examine the reasoning behind particular outputs and query models.

Assuring traceability for review and auditing

Every stage of the AI lifecycle is documented and made available for analysis thanks to traceability. Sustaining accountability and compliance requires this.

Important traceability features include:

1. **Version Control:** Monitoring modifications to setups, datasets, and algorithms.
2. **Decision Logs:** Documenting the inputs, outputs, and processing stages for each AI system decision.
3. **Incident Reporting:** Documenting information about irregularities, mistakes, or unfavorable results in order to guide remedial measures.

A healthcare AI governance platform, for instance, might record each patient diagnosis recommendation together with the data and model version utilized, allowing for a comprehensive review in the event that an error occurs.

In order to effectively control AI, this chapter emphasizes the significance of integrating strong accountability systems with ethical standards and legal frameworks. Organizations can implement AI ethically and build societal trust while achieving operational and regulatory objectives by taking these factors into consideration.

CHAPTER 3

ESTABLISHING TRANSPARENCY TO FOSTER TRUST

In order to ensure accountability, promote ethical use, and build trust, transparency in artificial intelligence (AI) is crucial. Decision-making processes are increasingly incorporating AI systems, and stakeholders—from users to regulators—demand that the workings of these systems be made clear. The function of explainability, open reporting, and stakeholder involvement in fostering trust via transparency is examined in this chapter.

3.1 AI Systems Explainability

Methods for Creating Interpretable AI Models

Designing AI systems that offer comprehensible and transparent insights into their decision-making procedures is known as explainability. Depending on the target audience and model complexity, several explainability strategies are used.

Typical methods include of:

The process of determining which inputs have the greatest impact on the AI's output is known as "feature importance analysis." Tools such as SHAP (SHapley Additive exPlanations) and LIME (Local Interpretable Model-agnostic Explanations) are frequently used to display this technique.

- Decision trees are simplified models that make judgments easy to follow by breaking them down into a series of if-then rules.

- The use of interpretable models, such linear regression, to mimic intricate systems, like neural networks, and produce insights that are comprehensible to humans is known as "surrogate modeling."

- **Counterfactual Explanations:** Giving consumers insight into the sensitivity and behavior of the model by showing how small adjustments to the input data would impact the AI's output.

Balancing Complexity with Clarity:

- Explainability is important, yet it can be difficult to

achieve without compromising the functionality of sophisticated AI systems.

- Simpler models, like decision trees, are simpler to explain, but they might not be as predictive as more sophisticated algorithms, like deep learning. On the other hand, complex models could be more accurate but more difficult to understand.

- **Hybrid Approaches:** Using interpretability tools, like heatmaps for convolutional neural networks (CNNs) in image recognition tasks, in conjunction with high-performing models.

- Customizing explanations for various stakeholders is known as "audience-specific explanations." For example, end consumers need high-level summaries, while developers could need in-depth algorithmic insights.

Businesses may guarantee transparency without sacrificing performance by incorporating explainability into AI design and maintenance.

3.2 Open Communication and Reporting

Building User-Friendly Reports and Dashboards

- Providing consumers and stakeholders with understandable, actionable information regarding AI systems is known as transparent reporting.

- Real-time insights into AI performance, decision-making procedures, and system status are provided by interactive dashboards. Important characteristics include:

- Accuracy, precision, recall, and other KPIs that are pertinent to stakeholders are examples of performance metrics.

- Visual warnings for any biases found during operation are known as Bias Indicators.

- **Audit Trails:** Records of the AI's choices and the evidence that supports them.

- Enabling stakeholders to create customized reports that cater to certain operational or regulatory requirements is known as "customizable reporting." A healthcare AI dashboard, for instance, might have simplified summaries for hospital executives and comprehensive patient outcome statistics for regulators.

Providing Stakeholders with Information That Is Accessible

Transparency is based on communication. Strategies that work include:

- **Simplified Language:** Information is presented in simple, intelligible language, avoiding jargon.
- **Visual Aids:** Using flow diagrams, infographics, and charts to efficiently and rapidly communicate difficult ideas.
- **Multimedia Tutorials:** Providing interactive modules and films to describe AI technologies and procedures.

A financial institution using AI for credit assessment, for instance, might offer a clear explanation of how variables like income and repayment history affect loan approvals.

3.3 Establishing Trust with Stakeholders

Examples of Effective Transparency Programs

The greatest way to illustrate transparency is using instances from everyday life. Case studies demonstrate how businesses have effectively used open and honest procedures to foster trust.

Microsoft's Responsible AI Initiative is one example.

Microsoft created its AI transparency guidelines and resources to guarantee responsible implementation. The following are some of the company's transparency initiatives:

- The AI Fairness Checklist is a manual for reducing prejudice in the development process.
- A foundation for explainability in machine learning models is provided by the InterpretML Tool.
- **Engagement Programs:** Holding workshops with stakeholders and regulators to guarantee adherence to moral principles.

Second Example: Google's Model Cards and AI Principles

- In order to give stakeholders precise information about a model's intended usage, restrictions, and performance indicators, Google launched Model Cards. Users' confidence in Google's AI products has increased as a result of this campaign.
- Establish a benchmark for transparency

documentation in the industry.

Increasing Organizational and Public Trust in AI

- Widespread adoption of AI depends on organizational and public trust in the technology. The interests of various stakeholder groups must be addressed by transparency initiatives.

Techniques for establishing trust:

- Providing information about possible dangers, system constraints, and mitigation measures is known as "proactive disclosure."

- **Stakeholder Collaboration:** Including advocacy organizations, regulators, and end users in AI development processes to make sure their viewpoints are taken into account.

- **Feedback Mechanisms:** Creating avenues for users to voice issues or recommend enhancements.

An e-commerce platform that uses AI to make tailored recommendations, for instance, might give users the ability to see and modify the variables affecting their recommendations, strengthening user empowerment and trust.

Organizations may create solid foundations for the ethical and responsible deployment of AI by giving explainability, transparent reporting, and confidence-building measures top priority. Transparency strengthens the trust necessary for sustained innovation and cooperation in addition to improving operational success. Advanced frameworks and methods for operationalizing these ideas across sectors will be covered in later chapters.

CHAPTER 4

AI Systems Risk Management

An essential part of guaranteeing the safe, moral, and efficient implementation of artificial intelligence (AI) systems is risk management. The likelihood of negative effects rises as AI is incorporated more deeply into decision-making and critical services. To guarantee that systems function as intended and uphold stakeholder trust, risk management focuses on detecting, reducing, and preventing these problems. This chapter explores the various hazards that AI entails, how to mitigate them, and how governance platforms contribute to sound risk management procedures.

4.1 Recognizing AI Dangers

Risk Types in AI Development and Implementation

Risks associated with AI can appear at different phases of development and implementation. In general, these risks can be divided into three groups:

1. Technical Risks:

- **Model Performance Issues:** AI models may fall short of reliability or accuracy standards, resulting in inaccurate forecasts or judgments. When an AI diagnoses medical disorders, for instance, it may incorrectly identify diseases, leading to treatment suggestions that are not appropriate.

- **Overfitting and Underfitting:** Inadequately trained models may perform less well in real-world situations due to either overfitting, which involves the model adapting excessively to training data, or underfitting, which involves the model failing to recognize important patterns.

- **Data Risks:** Incomplete, biased, or poor-quality data can undermine AI's ability to function, resulting in incorrect outputs or the reinforcement of systemic biases.

2. Risks to Ethics

- **Bias and Discrimination:** AI programs that have been trained on biased datasets have the potential to reproduce or magnify injustices. Hiring algorithms that have been educated on historical data, for example, could unintentionally give preference to particular demographics over others.

- **Privacy Violations:** When sensitive user data is misused or collected in excess, privacy rules may be broken and trust damaged.

- **Autonomy and Manipulation:** AI systems that improperly affect or control user behavior, like focused disinformation operations, raise moral questions.

3. Risks to Operations and Strategy

- **System Failures:** Unexpected AI system crashes or outages might interfere with vital functions like autonomous car navigation or real-time financial trading.

- **Cybersecurity Threats**: AI systems are susceptible to assaults, including data breaches that reveal private information or hostile inputs that alter model outputs.

- **Reputational Damage:** Transparency failures, moral transgressions, or non-compliance with regulations can cause serious harm to one's reputation.

Governance Platforms' Function in Risk Assessment

Platforms for AI governance are essential for methodically recognizing these threats. They offer:

- Comprehensive risk frameworks are pre-established risk classifications that are suited to particular sectors and uses.
- Data quality audits are instruments for evaluating the fairness, diversity, and integrity of datasets.
- Algorithms that find weaknesses in AI systems throughout the design, training, and deployment stages are known as automated risk analysis.

Organizations can perform proactive risk assessments with the help of governance systems, guaranteeing that possible problems are resolved before they become more serious.

4.2 Operational Risk Mitigation

Mechanisms for Monitoring and Intervention

Operational risks necessitate ongoing observation and

quick reaction plans. Platforms for effective governance include the following mechanisms:

1. Real-Time Monitoring

- **Performance Dashboards:** Centralized dashboards monitor metrics in real-time, including error rates, latency, and model accuracy.

- **Behavioral Drift Detection:** Recognizing instances in which models depart from anticipated behavior as a result of shifting inputs or external circumstances. An AI that does predictive maintenance, for instance, might behave differently as it encounters new kinds of machinery.

2. Alert Systems

- **Threshold-Based Alerts:** When metrics surpass or fall below predetermined thresholds, alerts are triggered. For example, the development team may be prompted to look into the root cause if a customer support chatbot exhibits higher error rates in its responses.

- In order to minimize false positives and guarantee that warnings are relevant and actionable, advanced platforms are able to evaluate the context of abnormalities.

3. Mechanisms with Humans in the Loop

Platforms for AI governance enable human control in crucial activities, allowing:

- In an emergency, the capability to stop or modify AI decision-making processes is known as "Manual Overrides."
- Requiring human approval for high-stakes choices, like approving a medical treatment or rejecting a loan application, is known as a validation pipeline.

Anomaly Detection and Response Tools

To identify and manage operational risks, anomaly detection tools are crucial. These consist of:

- **Statistical Tools:** Algorithms that identify anomalous data patterns or outliers, such as moving averages and Z-score analysis.
- **Machine Learning Models**: Unsupervised learning methods that detect anomalous system behavior, like autoencoders and clustering.
- **RCA (Root Cause Analysis):** Teams can identify

the cause of abnormalities and create workable solutions with the aid of platforms that provide RCA tools.

Organizations can minimize disruptions and preserve operational integrity by proactively addressing problems through the integration of these tools.

4.3 Handling Risks to Reputation

The role that governance plays in averting scandals

Ethical transgressions, data breaches, or system malfunctions can all pose reputational risks, which could result in regulatory scrutiny, public outrage, and a decline in customer trust. Strong governance frameworks are essential for reducing these risks since they:

- Integrating justice, accountability, and transparency into AI operations is one way to ensure ethical standards. Platforms might include bias-testing tools, for instance, to find biased results prior to system deployment.
- **Encouraging Communication:** Giving stakeholders, such as consumers, authorities, and the

media, understandable and understandable explanations of AI decision-making procedures.

- **Maintaining Compliance:** Constant observation guarantees compliance with international laws like the CCPA or GDPR, lowering the possibility of legal issues.

Proactively Addressing Ethical Vulnerabilities through Platforms

Platforms for governance provide preventative steps to guard against moral and reputational harm.

1. Identification and Mitigation of Bias

- Automated tools that check for bias across different demographic groups and highlight possible inequalities are known as Bias Testing Frameworks.
- **Algorithmic Adjustments**: Instantaneous suggestions for addressing model biases and guaranteeing fair results.

2. Accountability and Transparency

- **Audit Trails**: Detailed records of AI decision-making procedures that enable businesses to prove responsibility in the course of inquiries.

- Customized summaries of AI performance, ethical adherence, and risk management techniques that boost public trust are provided in Stakeholder Reports.

3. Procedures for Crisis Management

Platforms for governance incorporate crisis response features like:

- **Incident Reporting Systems:** Enabling prompt issue resolution and communication.
- Scenario simulations are tools that help organizations get ready for the worst-case situations, like major data breaches or system failures.

Case Study: Restoring Credibility Following Unethical Behaviors

- Think about a multinational bank using AI to score credit. Accusations of discrimination against minority groups resulted from a lack of bias checks. The organization used a governance platform to put in place thorough bias detection checks.
- Initiatives for transparency, such as disclosing

fairness measures to the public.

- Programs for engaging customers to restore confidence.

These actions improved the institution's long-term credibility in addition to reducing harm to its reputation.

A complex strategy including risk detection, mitigation, and proactive measures is necessary for effective risk management in AI systems. The foundation of these initiatives are governance platforms, which provide the instruments and structures necessary to guarantee that AI functions in an ethical, open, and trustworthy manner. Organizations may successfully negotiate the challenges of AI adoption while upholding regulatory compliance and stakeholder trust by thoroughly addressing operational, ethical, and reputational concerns.

CHAPTER 5

PUTTING AI GOVERNANCE POLICIES INTO PRACTICE

Converting concepts and principles into practicable, quantifiable, and legally binding procedures is the process of operationalizing AI governance policy. Making sure AI technologies are implemented ethically and in accordance with corporate objectives and legal requirements is an essential first step. This chapter examines the process of creating, putting into practice, and overseeing AI governance regulations, stressing the significance of flexibility and responsibility.

5.1 Creating Successful Policies

Frameworks for the Development of Responsible AI Policies

Creating policies that address operational, ethical, and legal issues while encouraging innovation is the cornerstone of successful AI governance. The following elements are commonly included in frameworks for the establishment of responsible policies:

1. AI Ethics Principles:

- **Fairness:** Regulations should guarantee that AI systems are just and do not reinforce prejudice or discrimination.
- **Transparency:** All parties involved, including users, staff, and regulators, must be able to comprehend how AI works.
- **Accountability:** Ethical deployment of AI requires clearly defined duties for its results.

2. Evaluation of Risk

A comprehensive grasp of potential dangers is necessary for effective policies:

- Establishing policies for anomaly identification, system malfunctions, and performance deterioration are examples of operational risks.
- **Ethical Risks:** Dealing with prejudice, privacy, and equity concerns.
- **Strategic Risks**: Maintaining adherence to changing

legislation and protecting the organization's reputation.

3. Involvement of Stakeholders

Designing inclusive policies entails involving a variety of stakeholders in order to get a broad range of viewpoints:

- Executives, legal teams, data scientists, and AI engineers are examples of internal stakeholders.
- End users, authorities, and advocacy organizations are examples of external stakeholders.
- **Cross-Industry Collaboration:** To improve governance, learn from other industries' best practices.

Assuring Conformity to Organizational Principles

The mission and basic values of an organization must be reflected in and upheld by AI governance policies. Policies that are aligned support long-term corporate goals like sustainability, innovation, and consumer pleasure.

- Encourage stakeholder trust by placing a high value on openness and moral behavior.
- Addressing the effects of AI on society will improve

corporate social responsibility.

Companies can accomplish this alignment by:

- **Value Audits**: Regular evaluations to make sure policies continue to be in line with company objectives.
- **Ethics Committees**: interdisciplinary teams that assess AI projects and offer policy suggestions.

5.2 Putting Governance Platforms into Practice

Complementing Current AI and IT Infrastructure

A smooth integration of governance policies with an organization's current workflows and systems is necessary for their successful operationalization. This includes:

1. Compatibility Assessment:

- **System Interoperability:** Verifying that governance platforms function with modern AI technologies, including data storage systems, monitoring tools, and machine learning frameworks.
- **Customizability:** Modifying platforms to satisfy the

particular requirements of the company while abiding by industry norms.

2. Allocation of Resources:

- **Dedicated Teams:** Determining roles and duties for governance platform implementation and upkeep.
- **Budgeting:** Setting aside funds for infrastructure improvements, platform licenses, and training.

The Best Methods for a Smooth Deployment

Organizations should adhere to these best practices to reduce implementation-related disruptions:

1. Phased Rollout

- To verify platform functionality and pinpoint areas for enhancement, start with pilot initiatives.
- Extend rollout gradually throughout projects and teams, taking input into account at every turn.

2. Training and Onboarding

- Give staff members thorough instruction so they can comprehend the platform's functionalities and their responsibilities in governance.

- Throughout the transition, provide continuing assistance to answer queries and overcome obstacles.

3. Integration with Workflows

- To expedite adoption, include governance duties like bias audits or compliance checks into current workflows.
- Utilize automation to boost productivity and decrease manual labor.

4. Stakeholder Communication

- Keep stakeholders updated on the goals, advantages, and developments of the governance platform's deployment through Stakeholder Communication.
- Resolve issues and take criticism into account to foster collaboration and trust.

5.3 Observation and Assessment

Methods for Continuous Policy Performance Evaluation

Continuous monitoring and assessment are necessary for effective governance in order to guarantee that policies continue to be applicable and efficient in changing contexts. Important methods consist of:

1. KPIs, or key performance indicators

Establishing and monitoring KPIs in line with governance goals:

- **Accuracy Metrics:** Assessing AI models' performance in comparison to standards.
- **Compliance Rates:** Monitoring compliance with company policies and legal obligations.
- **Incident Frequency:** Tracking instances of moral or practical problems, such prejudice or malfunctions in the system.

2. Loops of Feedback

- **Internal Feedback:** Gathering opinions from staff members and groups working on AI creation and implementation.
- Involving users and other stakeholders to gauge how governance policies affect their experiences is known as "external feedback."

3. Regular Inspections

Frequent audits aid in assessing how well governance procedures are working:

- **Ethics Audits:** Evaluating AI systems' accountability, transparency, and fairness.
- Finding weaknesses and making sure that strong data protection mechanisms are in place are the goals of security audits.
- **Performance Audits:** Examining model results to make sure they match company objectives.

Adaptive Governance Tools for Changing Environments

Tools that allow businesses to adjust to changing conditions, such revisions to regulations, technological breakthroughs, or changing stakeholder expectations, must be included in governance systems. Among these tools are:

1. Dashboards for Real-Time Monitoring

- Give a thorough overview of the risk indicators, compliance status, and AI system performance.
- Facilitate prompt issue detection and resolution.

2. Automated Policy Updates

- Support the adoption of new rules or moral principles by means of automated procedures.
- Minimize the time and work needed to change policies for various projects and teams.

3. Scenario Simulation

- Evaluate the possible effects of policy or external factor changes using predictive modeling.
- Encourage well-informed decision-making by weighing various approaches prior to execution.

4. Adaptive Algorithms

- Use machine learning methods to enable governance tools to gain knowledge from previous events and get better over time.

Organizations can guarantee that their governance procedures continue to be efficient, adaptable, and in line with changing demands by utilizing these instruments.

For enterprises looking to safely utilize AI's benefits,

operationalizing AI governance standards is a difficult but necessary process. Organizations may successfully manage the difficulties of deploying AI while promoting trust, compliance, and creativity by creating efficient policies, putting in place strong governance platforms, and regular monitoring and assessment of their performance. These initiatives set the stage for morally and sustainably sound AI procedures that complement business objectives and public norms.

CHAPTER 6

DATA PRIVACY AND AI GOVERNANCE

Since the reliability and effectiveness of AI systems are directly impacted by the ethical and legal treatment of data, AI governance and data privacy are closely related. The relationship between governance methods and data privacy is examined in this chapter, with particular attention paid to managing sensitive data, complying with regulations, and striking a balance between privacy and innovation. These components work together to provide a responsible AI system.

6.1 AI and Data Protection Laws

Data privacy problems have increased due to AI's expanding use across a variety of businesses. Regulations like the California Consumer Privacy Act (CCPA) and the General Data Protection Regulation (GDPR) have a significant impact on how businesses handle data in AI systems.

GDPR, CCPA, and Other Regulations' Effects

1. The General Data Protection Regulation, or GDPR, is the first

- GDPR, which was put into effect in the EU, places a strong emphasis on user control over personal data and requires businesses to: - Get express consent before processing personal data.
- Give users the option to see, edit, or remove their data.
- Data breaches should be reported within 72 hours.

Platforms for AI governance must incorporate capabilities that facilitate compliance, like automatic alerts for breach detection and audit trails for data usage.

2 The California Consumer Privacy Act (CCPA).

- Customers are granted rights under this California-specific law, including the ability to get information about the data that is gathered about them.

- Refusing to sell data.
- Asking for their data to be deleted.

By incorporating features for tracking, retrieving, and erasing data, governance platforms can uphold these rights.

3. Additional International Regulations

- **LGPD (Brazil):** Prioritizes consent and openness in data processing.
- **PIPEDA (Canada):** Prioritizes informed consent and accountability.
- **Indian Data Protection Bill:** Provides protections for handling sensitive and personal data.

Adhering to multiple regulatory requirements is a difficulty for organizations that operate internationally. By combining regulatory requirements into workable operations, governance platforms provide centralized solutions for preserving compliance.

Using Governance Platforms to Ensure Privacy Compliance

AI governance solutions facilitate compliance by:

- **Automating Data Audits**: Consistently assessing data processes to make sure they comply with relevant laws.
- Monitoring the how, when, and why of data usage in AI models is known as "tracking data usage."
- **Embedding Privacy by Design:** Promoting the incorporation of privacy safeguards across the whole AI development process.

Governance platforms guarantee that firms can manage data lawfully while lowering the risk of regulatory penalties by fusing cutting-edge technology with legal experience.

6.2 Handling Private Information

Because of its susceptibility and the possible repercussions of misuse, sensitive data such as financial information, health records, and personal identifiers needs to be protected with extra care.

Techniques for Encryption and Anonymization

There are two main methods for handling sensitive data effectively:

1. Encryption

Data is transformed into a secure code during encryption, which requires a particular decryption key to decode. Important characteristics include:

- Symmetric encryption, which offers faster processing but necessitates secure key distribution, uses the same key for both encryption and decryption.
- Using a public and private key pair, asymmetric encryption improves security at the expense of processing more slowly.

In order to prevent unwanted parties from accessing sensitive data, governance platforms incorporate encryption methods into data transfer and storage procedures.

2. Anonymization

Datasets are rendered useless for identifying reasons

through anonymization, which eliminates personally identifiable information (PII). Typical techniques consist of:

- Data masking is the process of hiding some fields in a dataset.
- **Generalization:** lowering the accuracy of data attributes, like substituting age ranges for birthdays.
- The creation of synthetic datasets that resemble actual data but do not include sensitive information is known as Synthetic Data Generation.

Anonymization solutions are incorporated into governance systems to facilitate model training and safe data sharing without sacrificing privacy.

Platforms' Function in Safe Data Management

Platforms for governance offer a complete approach to handling sensitive data by offering:

- **Access Controls:** Limiting authorized personnel's access to data according to their jobs and responsibilities.
- **Audit Logs:** Preserving documentation of data

access or modification, guaranteeing responsibility.

- **Real-Time Monitoring:** identifying anomalous behavior or illegal access and setting off alarms.

Governance platforms guarantee the safe and transparent handling of sensitive data throughout the AI lifecycle by integrating these features.

6.3 Harmonizing Privacy and Innovation

Encouraging innovation while maintaining strict privacy rules is one of the biggest problems in AI development. Maintaining stakeholder trust and encouraging the ethical deployment of AI depend on finding this equilibrium.

Ethical Innovation Strategies

The following strategies can help organizations achieve ethical innovation:

1. Technologies for Preserving Privacy

- **Federated Learning:** Enables AI models to be trained on distributed data without moving it to a central repository.

- **Differential Privacy:** Adds noise to datasets to keep people from being identified while maintaining analytical usefulness.

2. Boards for Ethical Review

- Innovation that is in line with societal values is ensured by forming interdisciplinary teams to assess AI initiatives for any privacy threats and ethical issues.

3. Development Through Iteration

- Organizations can continuously improve their AI systems by using an agile strategy, taking into account stakeholder input, privacy evaluations, and technical developments.

Building Trust Through Governance Tools Without Suppressing Creativity

Platforms for governance are essential for promoting responsible innovation since they:

1. Offering Privacy Metrics

- Monitoring adherence to privacy guidelines during the development phase.
- Pointing out places where privacy safeguards should be strengthened.

2. Facilitating Stakeholder Engagement:

- Providing transparency by means of reports and dashboards that convey governance procedures and data practices.
- Establishing confidence with partners, regulators, and users by showcasing a dedication to privacy.

3. Encouraging Collaboration

- Motivating interdisciplinary groups to work together to create AI solutions that strike a balance between creativity and privacy.
- To improve best practices, external views from industry, academia, and regulatory agencies are integrated.

4. Adapting to Change

- Providing scalable and adaptable governance

solutions that allow firms to react swiftly to changing privacy laws or technology advancements.

Case Studies: Juggling Innovation and Privacy

- **Healthcare:** To create predictive models for patient outcomes while adhering to HIPAA standards, a hospital network used federated learning.
- **Retail:** To evaluate consumer activity without jeopardizing user identity, an e-commerce platform implemented differential privacy approaches.
- **Finance:** To ensure transparency and regulatory compliance, a bank incorporated governance tools to track data consumption in AI-driven fraud detection systems.

Platforms for AI governance are crucial for managing the intricate connection between innovation and data privacy. Organizations may create AI systems that are trustworthy and valuable by following data protection regulations, handling sensitive data appropriately, and encouraging ethical innovation. Businesses can guarantee that their AI initiatives are both compliant and progressive in a rapidly changing environment by using proactive governance.

CHAPTER 7

GOVERNANCE OF AI THROUGH ETHICAL FRAMEWORKS

Artificial intelligence governance is based on ethical frameworks, which guarantee that AI systems are both responsible and effective. The values, norms, and procedures that characterize ethical AI governance are examined in this chapter. Organizations can develop AI systems that support society values and build stakeholder trust by emphasizing human-centric design, adhering to international standards, and encouraging diversity and inclusion.

7.1 Responsible AI Principles

The ethical and sustainable design, implementation, and management of AI systems are guided by the responsible AI principles. Prioritizing human wellbeing, tackling societal issues, and encouraging accountability in AI-driven decision-making processes are the main goals of these principles.

Ethical Decision-Making and Human-Centric Design

1. Design with Humans in Mind

In order to ensure that technology is a tool for empowerment rather than harm, AI systems must put human needs first. This comprises:

- Designing AI systems that comprehend and take into account a range of user experiences is known as "empathy-driven solutions."

- **Accessibility:** Designing features and user interfaces that people with disabilities or low technical skills can use.

- **User Autonomy:** Making sure users have the ability to govern AI results, including the ability to override or opt out of automatic judgments.

2. Making Ethical Decisions

Every phase of the AI lifecycle should incorporate ethical decision-making into AI governance platforms. This includes:

- **Assessing Impacts:** Analyzing how AI systems

might affect society and stakeholders.

- **Preventing Damage:** proactively recognizing and reducing hazards to susceptible groups.
- **Preserving Dignity:** Making certain AI applications adhere to human rights, freedom, and privacy.

Through the integration of ethical decision-making and human-centric design into governance platforms, companies can harmonize technology innovation with the welfare of society.

Including Accountability, Transparency, and Fairness

For AI systems to function responsibly, the FAIR principles Fairness, Accountability, and Transparency are crucial:

Fairness:

- Ensuring that all demographic groups are treated equally.
- Preventing unfair consequences by addressing algorithmic bias.

Accountability:

- Clearly defining who is responsible for choices pertaining to AI.
- To track and clarify decision-making procedures, audit trails should be established.

Transparency:

- Giving interested parties easily available information on the operation of AI systems.
- Providing tools for explainability that help make complicated algorithms more understandable.

By offering instruments for performance audits, bias identification, and transparent stakeholder communication, governance platforms operationalize these ideas.

7.2 Guidelines and Standards for the Industry

Organizations look to industry standards and guidelines that specify best practices for governance in order to guarantee worldwide uniformity in moral AI practices. Respecting these guidelines promotes accountability, trust, and interoperability.

ISO and IEEE Standards Overview

1. ISO Standards

Frameworks for properly controlling AI systems have been created by the International Organization for Standardization (ISO), and they include:

- **ISO/IEC 22989:** AI terminology and concept guidelines that guarantee industry-wide uniformity.
- **ISO/IEC 24027:** Guidelines for bias in AI systems, providing methods for detecting, quantifying, and reducing bias.
- **ISO/IEC 23894:** AI risk management guidelines, including risk identification and mitigation strategies.

2. IEEE Standards

- With guidelines like these, the Institute of Electrical and Electronics Engineers (IEEE) highlights the moral ramifications of artificial intelligence.
- **IEEE 7010:** Metrics for evaluating how AI affects human welfare.
- **IEEE 7001:** Transparency in autonomous systems: ethical considerations.
- **IEEE 7003:** Guidelines for evaluating algorithmic

bias.

By offering an organized method for developing and implementing ethical AI, these standards help businesses create systems that are both efficient and accountable.

How Adherence Is Supported by Governance Platforms

Governance platforms play a crucial role in putting these principles into practice and ensuring that they are followed by providing:

- Compliance dashboards are centralized interfaces that monitor real-time alignment with IEEE and ISO standards.
- **Automated Reporting:** Programs that produce thorough reports to prove compliance in audits.
- **Training Modules:** Instructional materials to assist groups in comprehending and successfully implementing ethical standards.

Governance platforms make it easier to maintain ethical and regulatory compliance by integrating these features, freeing up enterprises to concentrate on innovation without compromising accountability.

7.3 Encouraging Inclusion and Diversity in AI

To guarantee that AI systems represent the needs and experiences of a global community, diversity and inclusion are essential. Ignoring these principles might result in skewed results, diminished trust, and lost chances for creativity.

Bias Identification and Mitigation Tools

When algorithms generate unjust results because of unbalanced training data, faulty presumptions, or structural injustices, bias in AI occurs. Strong tools and techniques are needed to address this:

1. Bias Detection techniques

To find differences in representation or treatment, governance platforms incorporate bias detection techniques that examine datasets and model outputs. Among the essential skills are:

- Evaluating whether particular groups are over- or

under-represented in training data is known as "demographic analysis."

- **Outcome Comparisons:** Assessing if forecasts or choices disproportionately benefit particular groups.

2. Techniques for Mitigating Bias

Following the identification of biases, platforms provide corrective tools like:

- **Rebalancing Datasets:** Making sure that different groups are represented proportionally.
- **Algorithmic Adjustments:** Changing models to lessen their dependence on delicate characteristics.
- **Regular Audits:** Constantly keeping an eye on performance to avoid biases resurfacing.

Governance platforms enable enterprises to develop AI systems that are more equitable and inclusive by incorporating these technologies.

Inclusive AI Practices Case Studies

The importance of encouraging diversity and inclusiveness in AI development has been shown by a number of organizations:

1. **Healthcare:** By integrating a variety of patient data, a medical AI platform improved outcomes for marginalized populations by addressing discrepancies in diagnosis accuracy.
2. **Recruitment:** By eliminating identifiers from resumes and giving skills-based tests priority, a hiring algorithm was developed to eradicate gender prejudice.
3. **Education:** By integrating content catered to various socioeconomic and linguistic backgrounds, an adaptive learning tool addressed cultural bias.

These case studies demonstrate how putting diversity first not only produces better ethical results but also increases AI systems' general efficacy and uptake.

Responsible AI governance is based on ethical frameworks, which make sure that technology is in line with company objectives and society values. Organizations may create systems that are not only efficient but also fair and reliable by embracing the ideas of responsible AI, following industry standards, and encouraging diversity and inclusion. By operationalizing these principles, governance platforms help enterprises confidently and clearly negotiate the challenges of AI ethics.

CHAPTER 8

AI GOVERNANCE PLATFORM TRENDS FOR THE FUTURE

Strong and flexible AI governance platforms are becoming more and more necessary as artificial intelligence (AI) is incorporated into every facet of contemporary society. Technological innovation, smooth integration with AI lifecycle management, and flexible responses to changing regulatory environments are characteristics of future developments in AI governance. This chapter examines these advancements and offers an outlook on how governance systems can change in the future to address emerging issues.

8.1 Advances in Technology for Governance

Because AI is developing so quickly, governance technologies must be both current and flexible enough to grow and change over time. New developments in governance technology have the potential to revolutionize how businesses monitor and control AI systems.

New Instruments for Adaptive Policy Administration

Static policies that are manually reviewed and updated are the foundation of traditional governance systems. But because AI systems are dynamic, their governance mechanisms must also be dynamic. Important developments in this field include:

Updates to the Policy in Real Time:

Real-time monitoring features are being added to governance platforms so that policies can be dynamically modified in response to anomalies or changing circumstances.

- For instance, a governance platform may automatically update privacy or data-handling regulations when an AI system detects changes in user behavior trends.

Policy Simulation Tools:

Before implementing policies, organizations can test them in virtual environments thanks to sophisticated simulation tools. This lowers the possibility of unanticipated outcomes and guarantees that governance plans work in a variety of situations.

AI-Driven Policy Recommendations:

Governance systems are able to evaluate large volumes of data using machine learning algorithms to propose policy changes that are customized to the requirements of an organization.

- This method speeds up the policy-refinement process and reduces human error.

Governance technologies can stay up with the constantly changing needs of AI systems by utilizing these techniques, guaranteeing that oversight is strong and pertinent.

AI's Function in Self-Regulating Systems

- AI systems that can regulate themselves are the next big thing in governance technology. These systems add a layer of independent supervision by using AI to oversee and control other AI applications.

- **Continuous Compliance Monitoring:** Without human assistance, self-regulating systems may keep an eye on AI applications to ensure they adhere to operational, legal, and ethical norms. For instance, if a self-regulating system notices a bias violation or a violation of privacy rules, it may stop an algorithm from operating.

- **Adaptive Learning:** By integrating lessons learned from previous incidents or modifications to regulatory requirements, these systems employ adaptive learning approaches to gradually enhance their governance skills.

- In order to establish a cohesive supervision ecosystem and improve coordination and uniformity within an organization, self-regulating systems can be integrated with other governance platforms.

The creation of self-regulating systems is still in its early stages, but it has enormous potential to improve and streamline AI governance.

8.2 AI Lifecycle Management Integration

Platforms must smoothly interface with all phases of the AI lifecycle, from development to deployment and continuous operation, in order to accomplish full governance. By ensuring that governance procedures are ingrained throughout the procedure, this integration fosters responsibility and cooperation.

End-to-End AI Governance Supporting Platforms

In order to handle the particular difficulties at every phase of the AI lifecycle, contemporary governance platforms are developing to offer end-to-end support:

Development Stage:
- Platforms support ethical design throughout development by offering instruments for fairness testing, bias identification, and data quality analysis.
- Before using potentially discriminatory datasets for model training, for example, a governance platform may alert them.

Deployment Stage:

- Platforms monitor outputs in real time and flag anomalies that could point to policy violations in order to assure compliance throughout deployment.
- Features for automated reporting assist firms in proving compliance to stakeholders and regulators.

Operational Stage:

- During this stage, governance platforms offer ongoing supervision, which includes performance tracking, recurring audits, and necessary policy revisions.

Platforms assist enterprises in maintaining a consistent and proactive approach to AI supervision by providing governance throughout the full lifecycle.

Multidisciplinary Teams' Collaborative Tools

Data scientists, ethicists, legal professionals, and corporate executives must all contribute to AI governance, which is by its very nature a multidisciplinary process. For these varied parties to effectively communicate and coordinate, collaborative tools are crucial.

- Teams can access real-time data, policy updates, and compliance reports through centralized dashboards that are provided by governance platforms.
- All stakeholders are guaranteed to be working from a common knowledge basis thanks to these dashboards.

The following are examples of role-based access controls:
- Platforms provide role-based access controls to provide security and clarity, enabling each team member to view and edit just the data pertinent to their duties.

Integrated Communication Channels:
- Teams can work together without ever leaving the platform thanks to built-in communication features including document-sharing and chat systems.

In addition to increasing efficiency, these collaborative elements guarantee that a variety of viewpoints are considered when making governance decisions.

8.3 Getting Ready for Changing Regulatory Environments

As countries and international organizations strive to solve new issues, the regulatory landscape for AI is continuously evolving. To ensure long-term compliance and trust, governance platforms need to be built with the ability to anticipate and adjust to these changes.

Experiencing Upcoming Legal Difficulties

The following developments in AI regulation are anticipated to influence governance going forward:

Stricter Data Privacy Laws:

- As public awareness of data privacy increases, new jurisdictions are expected to adopt and enhance laws like the California Consumer Privacy Act (CCPA) and the General Data Protection Regulation (GDPR).
- To satisfy these changing needs, governance platforms need to include sophisticated privacy

management features.

Algorithmic Accountability Mandates:

- Organizations may be required by future rules to give thorough justifications of the judgments made by their AI systems.
- To meet these requirements, platforms must have strong explainability features.

Global Standardization Efforts:

- International organizations, like IEEE and ISO, are attempting to develop standardized AI governance frameworks.
- To be competitive and compliant, organizations need to make sure that their governance procedures follow certain international standards.

Governance tools can assist firms in confidently navigating complicated legal environments by staying ahead of regulatory changes.

Adaptive Governance in Environments That Change Quickly

Governance systems must be adaptable and sensitive to the rapid changes in regulations and technology. Important tactics for adaptive governance consist of:

- The process of scenario planning: Platforms might include tools for scenario planning that let businesses investigate the possible effects of new laws or advancements in technology.

- **Automated changes:** To guarantee that policies and procedures are up to date when rules change, governance platforms should have tools for automated changes.

- **Continuous Learning:** Machine learning can be used by platforms to assess patterns in the enforcement of regulations and offer proactive compliance advice.

Governance platforms can guarantee that businesses are ready for future uncertainty by adopting these flexible tactics.

Innovation, integration, and adaptation will determine the direction of AI governance platforms in the future. Dynamic policy management and self-regulating systems are made possible by emerging technologies, and thorough monitoring is ensured by seamless connection with the AI lifecycle. Adaptive governance techniques will be crucial for preserving compliance and confidence as regulatory environments continue to change. Organizations can establish themselves as leaders in moral and efficient AI governance by staying ahead of these trends.

CHAPTER 9

REAL-WORLD APPLICATIONS AND CASE STUDIES

The usefulness of AI governance's theoretical foundations depends on how well they work in practice. Examining how governance frameworks are applied in actual situations is necessary to fully comprehend their effectiveness. This chapter examines three crucial areas where AI governance has proven essential: healthcare, finance, and public sector applications. Every case study focuses on particular issues, governance tactics used, and the effects these have on creativity, trust, and compliance.

9.1 Healthcare AI Governance

The introduction of artificial intelligence is causing a revolutionary change in the healthcare industry. AI is improving medical results with individualized treatment plans and diagnostic tools. However, strong AI governance is crucial due to the sensitive nature of medical data and the moral ramifications of automated choices.

Protecting the Privacy of Patient Data and Ethical AI Use

Privacy is a major problem for healthcare businesses since they handle enormous amounts of sensitive patient data. Healthcare AI governance is centered on:

Encryption and Data Anonymization:

- Advanced governance tools guarantee that patient data is encrypted and anonymized prior to training AI models.
- Techniques for encryption reduce the chance of breaches by protecting data while it's in transit and at rest.

The General Data Protection Regulation (GDPR) in Europe and the Health Insurance Portability and Accountability Act (HIPAA) in the United States are two examples of legislation that governance systems must comply with.

- Healthcare businesses can detect and resolve possible infractions in real time with the use of automated compliance monitoring.

In order to guarantee that AI suggestions are in line with patient welfare, AI governance platforms integrate ethical norms into their decision-making processes.

- For example, evidence-based strategies that minimize damage and enhance benefit must be given priority in algorithms employed in cancer treatment.

Practical Illustrations of Medical AI System Governance

Healthcare AI applications have been effective thanks to governance frameworks:

The following:

- IBM Watson Health AI is used by IBM Watson Health to help with difficult disease diagnosis and treatment. Explainable algorithms, stringent data security measures, and adherence to medical rules are all part of its governance system.
- Watson for Oncology, for instance, offers explicit therapy recommendations that let doctors know why

each recommendation is made.

- **Google DeepMind with the NHS:** DeepMind collaborated with the National Health Service (NHS) of the United Kingdom to create the app Streams, which used artificial intelligence (AI) to forecast acute kidney injury. Stakeholder trust was restored when the partnership implemented stronger governance procedures, such as independent audits and public reporting, in response to early data privacy concerns.

These illustrations highlight the ways in which governance frameworks can promote innovation in healthcare while reducing risks.

9.2 Governance of the Financial Sector

One of the most highly regulated industries is finance, where artificial intelligence (AI) is essential to functions including lending, trading, and fraud detection. AI systems in finance run ethically, transparently, and within the law thanks to effective governance.

Controlling Hazards in AI-Powered Lending and Trading

The financial industry's AI-driven systems are particularly vulnerable to the following risks:

Lending Algorithm Bias:

- Governance platforms keep an eye out for biases in lending algorithms that can lead to discriminatory actions.
- Methods like counterfactual analysis ensure adherence to laws like the Equal Credit Opportunity Act (ECOA) by assisting in the identification and correction of unfair outcomes.

Risks of Market Manipulation:

- Algorithms for high-frequency trading (HFT) may unintentionally increase market volatility. Real-time monitoring is made possible by governance tools, which help identify odd trends and implement rules.

The following are some challenges in fraud detection:

- To prevent flagging legitimate transactions, AI models for fraud detection must strike a balance between precision and fairness. Model training is supervised by governance mechanisms to guarantee moral and useful results.

Transparency Case Studies in Financial AI Applications

Contract Intelligence (COiN) is a tool used by JP Morgan Chase to analyze legal texts using artificial intelligence. The governance structure guarantees that stakeholders comprehend the system's outputs by incorporating audit trails and explainability tools. JP Morgan improved operational efficiency while adhering to legal requirements by implementing these strategies.

Wealth Management Robotic Advisors:

- AI-powered robo-advisors are used by firms such as Wealthfront and Betterment to offer financial planning services. To foster client trust, governance frameworks incorporate regular audits and clear charge schedules. Additionally, these platforms follow fiduciary rules, guaranteeing that suggestions serve the interests of customers.

The banking industry has used AI to improve efficiency and decision-making while preserving client trust by implementing strong governance procedures.

9.3 Applications of AI Governance in the Public Sector

Adoption of AI in the public sector could boost decision-making, increase operational efficiency, and improve citizen services. Governance frameworks are essential, though, because the application of AI in government also brings up issues with accountability, equity, and transparency.

Establishing Government Services' Trust in AI

Building citizen trust must be a top priority for public sector AI applications by making sure:

Transparency in Decision-Making:

Governance platforms make it possible for AI systems

employed in contexts like social benefit distribution and tax assessments to be explained. For instance, the system should clearly explain its reasoning if an algorithm rejects a citizen's claim for benefits.

Mechanisms for evaluating AI choices and holding entities accountable for mistakes or biases are part of public sector governance systems.

- Decisions can be appealed or remedies can be sought through the proper means.

In order to make sure that AI implementations meet the needs and expectations of the general public, platforms include mechanisms for collecting citizen feedback.

Policies for Fair and Open Citizen Participation

Public sector governance frameworks prioritize the development of equitable policies, including:

- **Bias Mitigation:** To guarantee that all citizens are treated fairly, algorithms utilized in fields like recruiting and criminal justice are thoroughly examined for biases.

Governance platforms require tools like bias audits and fairness assessments.

- **Open Data Initiatives:** To improve openness, public sector organizations implement open data policies. Datasets used by AI systems are accessible to the public, encouraging accountability and confidence.

Instances of Governance at Work

AI in Policing:

- Los Angeles' predictive policing algorithms were criticized for reinforcing existing biases. Increased supervision, open reporting, and algorithmic fairness testing were among the governance measures. These actions decreased incidents of bias and increased community trust.

The e-Residency program in Estonia employs artificial intelligence (AI) to expedite government processes for digital entrepreneurs. Transparency, system security, and data privacy are prioritized in the governance framework.

- The program's operational and ethical objectives are met through regular audits and public feedback systems.

These case studies make it clear that fostering equity, accountability, and transparency in the public sector requires effective AI governance.

This chapter's case studies demonstrate how AI governance frameworks can be used to handle the particular opportunities and difficulties faced by various industries. Governance in healthcare guarantees the privacy of patient data and the moral use of AI. It improves openness and reduces risks in the financial industry. It fosters fair participation and trust in the public sector. Organizations can improve their governance practices and fully utilize AI while preserving ethical integrity and public confidence by taking lessons from these practical examples.

CHAPTER 10

AI GOVERNANCE'S OPPORTUNITIES AND CHALLENGES

In order to guarantee the moral, legal, and practical functioning of AI systems, AI governance has become essential. Despite its significance, companies have a difficult time successfully putting governance frameworks into practice. Simultaneously, there exist noteworthy prospects for augmenting AI governance via international cooperation, inventive metrics, and strategic stakeholder involvement. This chapter examines these difficulties and possibilities, offering a road map for businesses hoping to succeed in ethical AI governance.

10.1 Overcoming Obstacles in Implementation

There are challenges associated with the implementation of AI governance platforms. To achieve significant adoption, organizations need to solve organizational, cultural, and technical hurdles.

Difficulties in Implementing Governance Platforms

Adoption of governance systems may be impeded by various factors:

The integration of governance platforms with their current AI and IT infrastructure is a challenge for many enterprises. Inefficiencies may result from legacy systems' inability to accommodate contemporary governance tools due to their lack of compatibility.

- The answer is to use modular governance platforms that are compatible with a variety of systems and are scalable.

It can be challenging for smaller firms to invest in comprehensive governance solutions due to a lack of funding and experience.

- Solution: Organizations can pay for just the resources they require thanks to the affordable solutions provided by cloud-based governance tools.

Lack of Stakeholder Awareness: Stakeholders may

oppose adoption if they don't fully comprehend the benefits of AI governance and see it as an unneeded burden or expense.

- The answer is to arrange training sessions and workshops to inform stakeholders about the dangers of ignoring governance and the long-term advantages of putting strong frameworks in place.

Regulatory Ambiguity: Organizations may find it difficult to match their governance procedures with legal requirements due to the dynamic nature of AI legislation.

- The answer is to create adaptive governance systems that guarantee continuous compliance by integrating real-time updates on regulatory changes.

Tips for Successful Stakeholder Involvement

Organizations must actively include stakeholders at all levels in order to overcome these obstacles:

In order to guarantee that governance rules cater to a variety of demands, it is important to include members from IT, legal, operations, and leadership in the process of creating cross-functional teams.

- This strategy guarantees that policies are thorough and implementable while also fostering buy-in.

Including Stakeholder Feedback:

- Get opinions from staff members, clients, and other important stakeholders by using surveys and collaboration platforms.
- Feedback systems aid in finding governance weaknesses and coordinating policies with corporate objectives.

Showcasing Success Stories:

- Provide examples of effective AI governance deployments to illustrate observable advantages including increased efficiency, risk reduction, and trust.

Organizations may create the foundation for a successful adoption of AI governance by tackling these obstacles and successfully involving stakeholders.

10.2 Assessing Governance Success

To maintain the relevance and efficacy of policies, effective governance necessitates ongoing evaluation. Important phases in this procedure include creating precise measures and utilizing cutting-edge tools.

Metrics for Assessing the Results of AI Governance

Evaluating both quantitative and qualitative aspects is necessary to gauge the effectiveness of AI governance:

Compliance Rates:

- Monitor compliance with legal and ethical obligations, including data privacy regulations.
- High rates of compliance show that governance guidelines are successfully directing the creation and application of AI.

Decrease in Bias:

- Assess how much AI systems reduce biased results using fairness measures.
- Algorithms can function fairly if bias is found and

addressed through routine audits.

Transparency and Explainability:

- Evaluate how well AI systems explain their choices in a way that is easy to comprehend.
- Feedback from stakeholders can be used to gauge how transparent AI systems are thought to be.

Operational Efficiency:

- Assess how governance frameworks have improved operational procedures, such as quicker decision-making or lower error rates.

Confidence Metrics:

- Survey stakeholders to determine their level of confidence in AI systems. Perceptions that are positive show that governance frameworks are building trust.

Continuous Improvement Tools

Organizations can use adaptive governance techniques and tools to guarantee continued success:

Governance Dashboards:

- Real-time dashboards show areas for improvement while offering a thorough picture of governance performance. Organizations can respond swiftly to new hazards or inefficiencies thanks to these technologies.

Feedback Loops:

- Establish systems for routine stakeholder input to improve governance procedures and policies.
- Governance frameworks are kept in line with changing needs through iterative modifications based on input.

Benchmarking and Peer Reviews:

- To find best practices and areas for improvement, compare governance outcomes to peer organizations or industry standards.
- Collaborative reviews encourage innovation in governance tactics and the exchange of knowledge.

Organizations can make sure that their governance

frameworks provide long-term worth by concentrating on quantifiable results and utilizing cutting-edge solutions.

10.3 Prospects for International Cooperation

Global cooperation in governance has become crucial as AI systems increasingly cross national boundaries. Governance procedures can be harmonized with the aid of international collaborations and standards, guaranteeing uniformity and equity.

The Value of International Cooperation and Standards

A single framework for tackling cross-border governance issues is offered by global standards:

- **Harmonizing Regulations:** Multinational corporations may face compliance challenges because to variations in national AI laws.
- A common basis for governance processes is provided by international standards, like those created by the IEEE and ISO.

- **Advancement of Ethical AI:** The goal of cooperative projects like the Global Partnership on AI (GPAI) is to create standards that give ethical values like responsibility, transparency, and justice first priority.

Encouraging Knowledge Exchange:

- International conferences and forums allow organizations to exchange best practices and ideas, which promotes innovation in governance tactics.

Sites Promoting International Collaborations in Governance

International cooperation can be facilitated by governance platforms:

Cross-border compliance can be facilitated by platforms built with interoperability in mind, which can interface with governance frameworks in several jurisdictions.

Organizations can benefit from each other's experiences by using collaborative platforms that host shared datasets, algorithms, and governance regulations.

Global Monitoring Tools:

- Sophisticated monitoring systems are able to monitor adherence to global standards, guaranteeing that AI systems are in line with best practices around the world.

Instances of International Cooperation Initiatives

The OECD AI Principles are as follows: With an emphasis on sustainability, inclusion, and human rights, the Organization for Economic Co-operation and Development (OECD) has created guidelines for responsible AI.

- Frameworks for national and international governance are modeled after these ideas.

One of the most extensive regulatory frameworks, the European Union's AI Act places a strong emphasis on risk-based governance. Its clauses promote conformity to international norms, opening the door for international cooperation.

Organizations may promote equity, diversity, and creativity globally while navigating the challenges of AI governance by embracing global collaboration.

Platforms for AI governance are essential for handling the moral, legal, and practical issues raised by AI systems. Even though organizations encounter many obstacles when putting these frameworks into practice, these obstacles can be successfully overcome by strategic techniques like stakeholder engagement, quantifiable measures, and adaptive tools.

The chances for international cooperation highlight AI governance's revolutionary potential even more. Organizations can guarantee that AI systems benefit society by utilizing cutting-edge technologies, establishing international collaborations, and standardizing norms.

In the end, strong AI governance frameworks enable businesses to foster confidence, guarantee adherence, and responsibly unleash AI's full potential. Proactive governance will continue to be essential to moral and long-term AI development as the field develops.

ABOUT THE AUTHOR

 Author and thought leader in the IT field Taylor Royce is well known. He has a two-decade career and is an expert at tech trend analysis and forecasting, which enables a wide audience to understand complicated concepts.

Royce's considerable involvement in the IT industry stemmed from his passion with technology, which he developed during his computer science studies. He has extensive knowledge of the industry because of his experience in both software development and strategic consulting.

Known for his research and lucidity, he has written multiple best-selling books and contributed to esteemed tech periodicals. Translations of Royce's books throughout the world demonstrate his impact.

Royce is a well-known authority on emerging technologies and their effects on society, frequently requested as a speaker at international conferences and as a guest on tech podcasts. He promotes the development of ethical technology, emphasizing problems like data privacy and the digital divide.

In addition, with a focus on sustainable industry growth, Royce mentors upcoming tech experts and supports IT education projects. Taylor Royce is well known for his ability to combine analytical thinking with technical know-how. He sees a time when technology will ethically benefit humanity.